Gallery Books
Editor: Peter Fallon

A LIMERICK RAKE

Desmond O'Grady

A Limerick Rake

Versions from the Irish

Gallery Books

A Limerick Rake is published simultaneously in paperback and in
a clothbound edition by

The Gallery Press
19 Oakdown Road
Dublin 14, Ireland

© Desmond O'Grady. 1968, 1978

ISBN   0   902996   64   9   (cloth)
       0   902996   68   1   (paper)

Cover design by Michael Kane

The Gallery Press gratefully acknowledges the assistance of
An Chomhairle Ealaíon (The Arts Council of Ireland)
towards the publication of this book.

Contents

Made for
Ann and Barry Flanagan

A Limerick Rake

I am a young fellow that's aisy and bold,
In Castletown Conners I'm very well known,
In Newcastle West I spent many a night
With Kitty and Judy and Mary.
My father rebuked me for being such a rake
And spending my time in such frolicsome ways,
But I ne'er shall forget the good nature of Jane,
Agus fágaimid siúd mar atá sé.

My parents had reared me to shake and to mow,
To plough and to harrow, to reap and to sow
But my heart being too airy to drop it so low
I set out on a high speculation.
On paper and parchment they taught me to write
In Euclid and grammar they opened my eyes
And in multiplication in truth I was wise,
Agus fágaimid siúd mar atá sé.

If I chance for to go to the town of Rathkeale
The girls all around me do flock on the square,
Some buy me a bottle and others sweet cake
To treat me unknownst to their parents.
There is one from Askeaton and one from the Pike,
Another from Ardagh my heart has beguiled,
Though being from the mountains her stockings are white
And I'd like to be tightening her garters.

To quarrel for riches I ne'er was inclined
For the greatest of misers must leave them behind,
I'll purchase a cow that will never run dry
And I'll milk her by twisting her horn.
Feathery Bourke had plenty of gold,
His mother before him twenty times more,
But they're stretched on their backs among nettles and stones,
Agus fágaimid siúd mar atá sé.

This cow can be milked without clover or grass
For she's pampered with corn, good barley and hops,
She's warm and stout and she's free in her paps
And she'll milk without spancel or halter.

The man that will drink it will cock his caubeen
And if anyone cough there'll be wigs on the green
And the feeble old hag will get supple and free
Agus fágaimid siúd mar atá sé.

If I chance for to go to the market of Croom
With a cock in my hat and my pipes in full tune,
I'm made welcome at once and brought up to a room
Where Bacchus lies sporting with Venus.
There's Eileen and Jane from the town of Bruree
And Betty from Bruff and we all on a spree
Such a combing of locks as there was about me
Agus fágaimid siúd mar atá sé.

There's some say I'm foolish and more say I'm wise
But being fond of the women I think is no crime
For the son of King David had ten thousand wives
And his wisdom was highly regarded.
I'll till a good garden and live at my ease
And each woman and child can partake of the same
If there's war in the cabin themselves they may blame
Agus fágaimid siúd mar atá sé.

And now for the future I mean to be wise
And I'll send for the women that acted so kind
And I'll marry them all on the morrow by and by
If the clergy agree to the bargain.
And when I'm on my back and my soul is at peace
All the women will crowd for to cry at my wake
And their sons and their daughters will offer their prayers
To the Lord for the soul of their father.

Popular Irish Song

10

The making of this collection is something of an experiment. Ezra Pound said in *Notes on Elizabethan Classicists* that "a great age of literature is perhaps always a great age of translations". Throughout his long literary life he at all times stressed translation as one of the threads that link the individual talent to the poetic tradition. And translation, or imitation, in great literary periods is not necessarily a form of creation inferior to what we call *original writing*. The same conditions are necessary for successful translation/imitation as for good poetry. Ben Jonson in his *Timber* said much the same: "The third requisite in our *Poet*, or Maker, is *Imitation*, to bee able to convert the substance of riches of another poet to his owne use". Ezra Pound also believed the literature of a country should be translated afresh every generation since the meaning of language changes so rapidly.

It is in this spirit that the poems in this collection are made. My intention has been to attempt to "make" a poem in English from the original language that I hope works as an English poem in its own right. To this end I have used different methods of composition to re-create the original. This has meant making an almost infinite series of changes in phrasing, feeling, tone, nuance, ornament and form. *The Poet and His Dog* derives from the famous medieval Irish poem *The Scholar and His Cat*. My *Kathleen, the Daughter of Houlahan* is an enlarged version of both Heffernan's original and James Clarence Mangan's translation combined. With the Raftery poems I have dropped several stanzas for the sake of tempo or urgency. I have taken much licence with the group of poems from the Irish love tradition in an attempt to get across their subtlety and sophisticated *double entendre* that is comparable with the Amour Courtois and Goliardic tradition of the Continent.

The Ossian poems from the Fenian Cycle were the most difficult to render in a readable form. Their form in Irish is extremely strict and to hold to it in English would greatly hamper the fluency of the original which is a dialogue between pagan Ossian, returned from the magical Land of Youth, and Christian Saint Patrick, leader of the new order in Ireland.

I have not dated the poems on the page, considering that a distraction from my purpose of making them stand as poems in English. However, their dates are as follows: the love poems were composed between 1200 and 1700 A.D.; the Ossian poems have their setting in the 3rd century and were written down between the 11th and 13th centuries. The other poems, except for Anthony

Raftery (1784-1835), come from the anonymous oral folk tradition and could have been written at any time between 1650 and 1850. The Celtic Sura is medieval. Patrick Pearse is 20th century. *Promised Land*, I'm told, was originally written in German and translated into Irish.

Acknowledgement is made to The Dolmen Press who published the first version of a number of these poems in *Off Licence*. In this collection they are variously revised. I wish to express my thanks to Antoinette Moses for her dedicated assistance in putting this book together.

My sole interest in making these poems is an experiment in artistic freedom in the form Ezra Pound would call creative translation.

Desmond O'Grady,
Naoussa, Paros, 1978.

The Poet Sends a Poem to his Love

A pleasure, my poem, for you to be
        seeing my lady's curled hair;
would I were you and you were me,
        then I myself would travel there.

I'm happy, my poem, today you'll be
        lying where my true love lies;
her calabrian red blood lips you'll see
        and see her flashing teeth and eyes.

The deep south of her eyes you'll see,
        what's more you'll touch her soft white hand,
alas, it's you, not I, will be
        beside the finest girl of the land.

You'll see my lady, fair and fine,
        and feel her brushed hair firelight bright;
you'll lie beside her body's line
        that I held in a dream last night.

You'll see her waist, untouched and slight,
        that's locked me in a lovestruck trance;
each foot bright-toed and marble white
        you'll see is full of lightening dance.

And you will hear her throaty voice
        strong as one straight cross-hatched line,
tragic, resonant, choice —
        I wish your luck now were mine.

A Weakness for Women

A weakness for women's
a welcome curse.
Too much may soften
our hardness of purpose,
but it's our aspiration
to rise to every occasion.

No matter how we wrinkle
it never ages.
While it can tease us
we'll never grow old.
Love in your hand
silvers your pocket.

Bed business's
the best business.

The Poet Loves from his Distance

I think now I'll whore it up for a while
and quit making out to be what I'm not.
Women with balls who'd cramp any man's style
make a dangerous lot.

Although it's women of wholesome structure
men on the make most want to bed,
there's a girl called Gormflah I'd like to fracture
and no word said.

If I had the pick of the ripest locals,
the hottest from here to the town of Maynooth,
a hammer at her would loosen my yokles,
stretched or stood up.

14

Woman Honour

Let's honour women,
treat them with leniency,
forgive their fault of secrecy.
They're human.

Honour them here tonight;
find no fault with their ways;
give them their due praise.
Even wrong, they're right.

Don't hold their history against them.
Forgive their treachery,
farce of fidelity —
accept them.

Ignore public opinion.
To my own bitter end
I'll never understand
anything about them.

The verse of those who knock
them's flat as common slate.
All we've achieved to date
we owe to their work.

The Poet Defends Women

Cock-cramped the man ridicules women.
Without them we'd never have poetry meetings.
No genuine woman was half the demon
we men call them in their dealings.

Their speech is gentle, their talk quick-witted;
they alone deserve idolatry;
to sour against them we're half-witted —
he's a foolish man questions their quality.

No treason or murder hardens their frailty,
to treacherous dealings they never play party;
of wrong to the church they don't stand guilty —
it's a foolish man questions their quality.

No one's been born except to a woman:
No bishop, priest, no member of royalty;
no chief of state, no crucified jew man —
he's a foolish man questions their quality.

They lock up the colours of love in their heart,
they like their men well-groomed and healthy.
A cornered man must play up his part —
he's a fool whoever questions their quality.

Some fat old greybeard whose shins' gone yellow
is the last they want in the dark for company;
but a big ballsed strapping, even penniless fellow
who'll test the metal that tempers their frailty.

The Love War

I'll tell you something for
nothing. There's no war
where more have died
than the love war. I'm surprised
I survived. I'll never give in
to any woman and, between
us, I'm the better for it.
I don't intend to change in that.

The men who die for love leave
their women behind alive.
Then they and the rest of us
have the time of our life
at their absent expense.

The fools die.
The wise survive.
Why die and leave
women alone to live?

The Creation of Courtship

My subject's the secret of courtship.
I'll tell it straight —
you should know its start:

That Kerry man's son
Dermot, nervous, skinny,
was the first man
to worship Grainne.

Then that cowboy Cuchullain
fell for a woman down
in Greece. Without Greek,
he invented the wink.

The son of Con Carney,
a thoroughbred upstart,
turned love to an art
by making a courtesy.

Then Neesha, a sportish fellow,
passed Deirdre near her house;
stopped, forgot to follow
the hunt, made up the kiss.

On the banks of the Boyne, MacOch,
stripped off his fashionable cloak,
dived in for his daily swim
and the druid's daughter with him.

The son of another king,
who couldn't box his corner,
invented sprinkling water
on any young skirt passing.

There was one dwarf,
I forget his name,
never did things by half,
thought up throwing flowers at women.

There's many a clever story
about young Dessie O'Reilley;
he practised the tear and the sigh
to get young girls to lie.

A well-known master tradesman
made use of all his craft
to change young virgins into women
before he upped and left.

You work on young girls
with tears in your eyes,
a sob in your throat,
your hand on that lute.

But I myself got stuck
with a bag of jealous stuff;
didn't dump it quick enough —
that's my tough luck.

Love's No Illness

Love's no illness.
We lie in this.
No healthy man
refused a woman.

When I'm in love
I howl on the job.
Far from killing, love
keeps me alive.

I'll play soft music,
won't get sick;
I'll feed the blood,
perfume the bed;

I'll tan my skin
for any virgin,
fresh and young
shaped like a swan.

I'm slow as a tree in a stream,
my tone of voice tells you that.
The lightest shawl casually thrown
on my shoulders, still feels hot.

No fire burns fiercer
than my flesh. No water-
fall or cold north sea
can cool me.

If that young lady
left me,
I'd definitely die
and quickly.

I'm straight as a spade,
upright as plumthread;
my thirst could empty a lake,
stone-hard my stomach.

I know day's not night,
can see black's not white,
I know a boot from a sod of turf
whether or not I'm in love.

I can tell a dog from a donkey,
smell the small from the big-fry;
I know the sea's no mountain,
that a whale won't fit in a fountain.

The screw of a ship out of the waves,
the thickness of trout without its scales
spell no more sense than the woman's name
that has me tied to her, ball and chain.

She's that one I want in particular.
I'll deny it here no longer.
But this does not derail me.
I suffer, but I'm easy.

Broken Love

It's long since my foot a shoe sported
and longer my pocket a penny;
many's the woman I've courted
but was never contented with any.

It's long my grave's in the making
and longer my feet on the move;
there's nothing but grief for the taking
since the day I broke with my love.

Abandoned Love

Lass fair and slight,
queen of the herd,
where are you by night
by day where heard?

I roamed with my lover
fields, woods and rivers;
now he's gone with another
and left me in tears.

I haven't got land
or music, or wine
or maids who attend,
or courtiers fine.

All the water is mine
to drink if I'm able,
while whiskey and wine
deck my enemy's table.

In the Greenwood

1

My darling, my love,
Together let's rove
Through the forest so fragrantly scenting.
By trout streams we'll rest,
Watch the thrush build her nest,
While the buck and the roe buck are calling.
Each ring singing bird
In the wild wind wood heard
And the cuckoo high up in the plane trees
And never will come
Death into our home
In the shade of the sweet smelling green-trees.

2 *Love Fragment*

O beautiful head
All kiss curled red,
Green and grand your eyes are;
My heart is high-strung,
Like a thread too well spun,
From loving too long from afar.

After Love

The stars stand upright in the sky.
Sun and moon together lie.
No hot drop's left in my salt wet eye.
No swan swims.

Three thoughts remain within me after love:
guilt, pain, my open grave,
the sense of someone slipping away,
limp lying limbs.

The Birds

How wonderful for birds,
they fly land and sea,
all together sing
in the branches of a tree.

It's not the same
for me and my love.
Farther from each other
we daily move.

Paler than the lily,
more delicate than spring;
she's sweeter than the violin
or any song you'll sing.

No language can describe her,
my words are all in vain;
O God, high in heaven,
release us from our pain.

The Spinning Wheel

Before we got married, this woman and I,
she'd make short work of six pounds of wool;
but after the wedding and I built our own place
she wouldn't have worked through a pound in a month.

Chorus: O my wife, my kids and my spinning wheel,
my pile of wool at home unspun;
she takes a week's rest for a day's work done;
dear God unhoist this weight off me.

I thought I had picked out the best of the locals.
She was gentle and graceful, had a face without fault;
but when I found out the worth of the woman
too late I realized the fool I was made.

Chorus: O my wife, my kids and my spinning wheel,
my pile of wool at home unspun;
she takes a week's rest for a day's work done;
dear God unhoist this weight off me.

When she sees me walk the road to the house
she quickly plants on a high pile of turf,
drives children and chickens wild through the place
and kicks the dead spinning wheel turning again.

Chorus: O my wife, my kids and my spinning wheel,
my bales of wool piled up unspun.
Tobacco in one palm, her pipe in the other
and never a thought where I'll find the rent.

I swear that I'll yet be the end of this woman.
I swear that I'll yet plant her ten feet under.
If I have to put up with her laziness longer
I'll swing from the gallows in three short months.

Chorus: O my wife, my kids and my spinning wheel,
my bales of wool at home unspun.
She'll take a week's rest for a day's work done.
O Christ untackle this saddle on me.

From *'THE FENIAN CYCLE'*

1 *Ossian to Patrick*

Here's one about Finn:
We numbered fifteen
no more; we knackered
a Saxon king from his kin
and shoved back some Greeks
to their ship on the shore.

We perennially plundered
the continent. On regular
raids we'd hit and get out —
in, win, out; that's
what we were about.
Hit from the White Sea
down to Bombay and ship
home their amber and gold.

Finn scored eight times
straight in Spain. The High
King of the Saxon's woman
lay down to his honour;
and our world reeled round
as no one has told
on the open road
at home and abroad.

2 *The Songbird*

There's a famous songbird
sings sweeter than starlight.
I'v never heard
such serene song. Patrick,
forget your church bells,
listen to that bird. Prayers
can wait for later.
If you hear that song at evening
you'll forget where we go
and why, after we die.

3 *Hills*

These boxwood hills
flash flush with wild
game, fructify wild
fruit, level off
in green grass meadow.

The country's finest,
these hills stand back
from our open sea. On
the one open eye side
our broken head of land,
the other our broken width of sea.

It's hard to leave here
for the strong city.

4 *Benn Aedar*

Stand up on Benn Aedar.
Look out on the linen stitched
sea. The man migrated mountains
fold, the each line drawn one
the other, houses hard worked at harvest.

Here hoist the hills
our Fianna met on;
ate, drank, danced on.
Free our fine fresh open
hills where gamesome Deirdre eloped
with fairheaded Grainne.

5 *The Fruit Tree*

I'd been on the move
three days without rations.
Finally I made it
to Madman's Gully.
A legendary fruit tree grows there.
They say one look at its fruit
suffices to satisfy any appetite.
I remember the last time we camped
there. We'd been on the hunt with Finn.
We brought him a bag of this fruit
and a brace of wild boar.

6 Ossian's Lament

Mine's a sad story, Patrick.
An old man in his dry age
left living alone. Too well
I hear the toll of your bell
in my withered heart.
If I could bring back again
those days with the Fianna
I'd leave you and your puny
pasty faced priests and head
for the hills again hunting and horseriding.

I hope your God has granted His Heaven
to Finn and my friends and will
to me in my time because if I've done
any man wrong, I regret it.

7 Finn's Wishes

Popular leader, national hero
his wishes were: praise for action,
the sounds of nature morning and evening,
rest by a waterfall, the hunt through the woods,
birdsong in the bushes, the wave's wash,
the chant of singers of stories,
the yelping of hounds at the hunt,
clatter of ravens on Skaldcrow Hill,
the stampede of venison on southern slopes,
the seagulls' glance glide off the cliffs' face,
cackle of circling crows in reply,
hauling home deer by the hind legs,
barking beagles round his knees,
and at night, round the fire, swapping stories.

Patrick:

Get up Ossian
        you've slept too long;
Though many's the mad
        noisy battle you've fought
Get up and hear
        the sweet psalm's song
Now you are grey,
        old and worthless.

Ossian:

I heard music
        before you came
far sweeter than any
        your choirs could sing:
The song of the bird
        from Letter Lane
and the powerful sound
        of the harp of Finn.

The song of the thrush
        from Glenn-a-Skald
And the sound of curraghs
        scraping on sand;
The barking of hounds
        is sweeter than all
The chanting of clerics
        in choir together.

Dirol's choice
        was the choice of my heart —
Dirol, the little
        dwarf harper of Finn —
When he played the song
        built into the harp
And all the many
        strong songs we sang.

The dozen goats
            that served Finn's tent,
When they ran loose
            in Ragman's Glenn,
Were sweeter than all
            your church sung hymns
As they grazed in the fields
            by the river Suir.

When Finn MacCumhail
            sat on the mound
The harp of Finn
            played without fault,
His brave band dozed
            at the beautiful sound,
A sound far finer
            than all your chant.

Raftery the Poet

I am Raftery the poet.
My two eyes stare blind;
I've known love, still hold hope,
live in peace of mind.

Weary and worn
I walk my way
by the light of my heart
to my death's marked day.

Look at me now,
with my arse to the wall,
playing for people
who have nothing at all.

The County Mayo

Now with the spring
        the days will stretch,
then after the Feast
        my feet will itch,
and I'll shuffle and shunt
        till I rise and go
and plant myself down
        in the County Mayo.

At first in Claremorris
        I'll stay, I'm thinking,
and in Balla below it
        I'll start my drinking;
from there on to Killty
        for a month or more,
then the last few miles
        to Ballinamore.

Well honest to God
        my heart whips up —
like the wind whips up
        and scatters the fog —
when I think of Carna
        or Balla below,
of the Gap o' the Bushes
        or the plains of Mayo.

In Killaden town
        there's everything good,
rich produce and fruit
        and all kinds of food;
and now if I stood
        among my kin
I'd feel, not old,
        but young again.

Anthony Raftery

The Lass from Ballynalee

On my way to Mass
        to say a prayer,
the wind was high
        sowing rain,
I met a girl
        with wind-wild hair
and madly fell
        in love again.

I spoke with learning,
        charm and pride
and, as was fitting,
        answered she:
"My mind is now
        well satisfied
so walk me back
        to Ballynalee."

Given the offer
        I didn't delay
and breaking a laugh
        with this willing young lass,
I swung with her over
        the fields through the day
till shortly we reached
        the rump of the house.

A table with glasses
        and drink was set
and then says the lassie
        turning to me:
"You're welcome Raftery,
        so drink a wet
to love's demands
        in Ballynalee."

I've walked in my time
        across England and France,
from Spain to Greece
        and back by sea;

met many a girl
            at many a dance,
but none had an airy
            grace like she.

If I had the power
            and the flower of youth,
I'd find her out
            wherever she'd be,
I'd comb all the coasts
            from Cork to Beirut,
to live with this gem
            from Ballynalee.

No matter her name,
            she's a well-bred lass,
with the looks and grace
            of the queen of a tribe;
looks two hundred scholars
            en masse,
or the pick of the poets
            could never describe.

Venus and Deirdre
            were no more grand,
nor Helen who launched
            the ships in the sea.
She's the brightest blossom
            of all Ireland,
this fabulous flower
            from Ballynalee.

My star of light,
            my autumn sun,
my curly head,
            my summer sky —
in Sunday's shadow
            let's rise and run
and arrange the place
            where we shall lie.

All I ask is to sing
          your say each Sunday night,
with drink on the table
          and you on my knee.
Dear God high in heaven
          who gives and takes sight,
grant me this grace
          in Ballynalee.

Anthony Raftery

Seán O'Dwyer

When I rose in the morning,
while the summer sun was shining,
I heard a far shout calling
     and the singsong of the birds;

heard hoof of hunting rider,
the crush of making cider,
the sound of spinning spider,
     blunt shots from fowling guns;

heard fox bark in the heather,
a thousand shouts together,
sour spinsters who felt better
     counting coins and gold.

Now they cut down trees each day,
I shall pack and go my way
since there's nothing I can say
     will bring back my levelled woods.

This is my greatest sorrow:
with the forests felled tomorrow
the wind will find my morrow
     and death cloud the sky.

My goat, held by a hobble,
will no more buck and tumble;
my neighbours fight and squabble
     from dawn to dusk each day.

Our hero's hearts lie fallow
from Donegal to Mallow
their lives and hearts gone hollow
     until the Judgement Day.

If I'm not left alone
by the people in the town,
to Galway I shall turn
     and quit this reckless squander.

The Valley of Running Water,
its woods stretched out for slaughter,
has no man's son or daughter
      to toast its rich harvest.

My body braves the storm
from Cluan to Stuire-na-Colum
While beasts of every form
      nightly howl the moon.

Who makes this curse on Galway
we witness night and day,
that makes the wren and jay
      go silent in the trees?

Yes we'll have war for sure
with our priests and people poor
and fishermen forced to moor
      their boats with empty nets.

It is my greatest sorrow
I can't emigrate tomorrow
and never see the famine
      that certainly will come.

O the summers I have been
in orchards and have seen
a thousand oaks in green
      and cobwebbed dew on grass.

It's a lonely road I bend
away from home and friend
and cold the nights I spend
      in caves among the hills.

If I'm not left alone
by those people from the town
I shall leave, for life, my own,
      my country and my race.

Donnagha White

This town witnessed the wrong of a nation
in Donnagha White and his condemnation;
hit hat the hood of those judged to die,
a hangman's noose his collar and tie.

I've rushed all night with no rest or sleep,
like a spring lamb lost in a flock of sheep,
with fear in my heart, mad fire in my head
to find my young brother already dead.

I mourned you first at the edge of the lake
and mourned you next at the gallows' stake,
I mourned again at the feet of your corpse
among the British and the British curse.

If I only had you among your own
in Ballinarobe or in Sligo town,
the scaffold they'd break, the rope they'd sever
and you'd walk home on your name and honour.

For no hangman's scaffold were you born,
but for reaping wheat and threshing corn,
for ploughing the top-soil left and right
and turning the red clay into sight.

Dead brother Donnagha, honest and true,
well I know those who betrayed you;
drinking and smoking and plotting all night
and stalking the dew at the day's first light.

You, Mulhall, who struck this blow
my brother was no thieving cow,
but an honest man in thin and in thick
who could knock a sweet tune from a hurling stick.

But Donnagha White, since the only truth
is the grandeur and grace of buckets and boots,
we'll lay you out in fine homespun
and send you off like a noble's son.

Mulhall, your sons were never united
and your daughters with dowries were never delighted!
Our table's swept bare, the white boards full
with my brother, dead from a hang-rope's pull.

I see Donnagha's dowry coming home
and it is not cattle nor crops of his own
but tobacco and pipes and the long candles' light
and no boast brightens our boy's black night.

Promised Land

Sailed a ship for foreign places;
Loosed her ropes and sailed away;
Still her painted name means to me
Lands of sun beyond the bay.

"Come," said she, "Come sail my waters;
Sail away from cloud and cold;
Come to metal blue of mountains,
Mirrored cities white as gold."

Full of hope and full of living;
Being young I would not sail;
I believed that I had part of
All that makes a poem or tale.

Sailed the ship across the ocean
Far from here, with masts of gold;
Wrote her name across the evening,
Down the sky in letters bold.

She will come and take me one day
To her promised land abroad;
I shall see white cities hoped for;
I believe still, almost, Lord.

If I Went Away

If I went away I should never come back,
but hike the hills, sound each hollow,
tramp the stony goat-herd track
and my own wild will happily follow.

My heart is as black as a burned door,
or the burnt out coal in a kitchen range,
or the stamp of a boot on a whitewashed floor
and memory makes my smile turn strange.

My heart in a thousand bits lies shattered
like broken ice on the water's face,
like a heap of stones you've knocked and scattered
or a virgin fallen in disgrace.

I shall leave this town as soon as I can;
sharp the stone here, deep the dung;
there's nothing of value here for a man
but the heavy word from everyone's tongue.

Prayer of the Woman of the House

Mother of Grace,
               mother of Christ,
That you may put
               all at their ease.

That you may save
               from every ill;
That you may save
               in body and soul.

That you may save
               on land and sea;
That you may save
               in time of pain.

Sentinel angel
               overhead;
God before
               and God behind.

The Irish Tongue

Munster Irish is a rich tongue
with a foreign tone from foreign aid;
a clear sound, clear as song,
crisp, clever, finely grained.

Though Hebrew they claim is the oldest
and Latin and Greek the most learned,
on none of them have we trespassed
for phrase or sentence no matter how worded.

Naked I Saw You

Naked I saw you,
Beauty's child.
I shut my eyes
not to yield.

I heard your song
call me near.
I covered my ears
not to hear.

I tasted your mouth,
sweetest of all.
I hardened my heart
not to fall.

I shut my eyes,
my ears I covered;
I hardened my heart,
desire I smothered.

I turned my back
on your embrace,
to the course I've set
I turned my face.

I turned my face
to the course I've set;
to what I'll do,
though it mean death.

Patrick Pearse (1879–1916)

Kathleen, the Daughter of Houlahan

With dreams burned out like cinders and spirits crushed like chalk,
the royal men of Ireland,
deprived of country, stalk
the palace courts and halls of foreign France and Spain
or, on some foreign strand,
beneath a foreign reign,
fight foreign nation's causes since forbad to fight their own.
But fast the day is coming
when the tyrant British Crown,
from every Irish acre and every Irish town,
will be driven out in warring
by the Royal Warrior Son
                     of *Kathleen, the Daughter of Houlahan.*

It will not now be long before the nation ring
a million bells of freedom
and a million throats will sing
and harp the many songs that are so long unsung —
throats so long struck dumb
singing in their native tongue.
Our exiled men returned, like birds in early spring,
among their kith and kin,
will also toast and sing
the ancient lays of Ireland and the freedom newly won
by him, our new born Finn,
the Royal Warrior Son
                     of *Kathleen, the Daughter of Houlahan.*

How many generations in every Irish home
have prayed that foreign nations
would in their warships come;
their thousand masts a forest against an Irish sky,
their guns no imitations,
their steel pikes eight feet high;
would come to free our country, a hundred thousand strong?
Our scholars look like scarecrows,
our poets sing no song;
with prices on their heads, our priests are on the run.
But our answer to our foes
is the Royal Warrior Son
                     of *Kathleen, the Daughter of Houlahan.*

The hair of Princess Kathleen is gold as autumn grain,
and all her gold-ring curls
fall like a gold-leaf train;
her eyes are sapphire lakes in mists of morning sun,
a gown of purple furls
a form for gods alone.
Her voice is pure as silver, with all the silver tone
of a love song on a hill
when the piper pipes alone.
To guard this ageless beauty is what has to be done
led by the warring skill
of the Royal Warrior Son
                    of *Kathleen, the Daughter of Houlahan.*

These tyrants who suppress us and think our spirit spent
will soon see justice done.
Soldiers will be sent
from friendly kings in Europe to help us in our need.
Good Virgin, ask your Son —
who led His chosen seed
of Israel free — to guide and give us courage
all through the battle hour.
And may He too encourage,
both young and old alike, to fight until we've won
his rightful kingdom for
the Royal Warrior Son
                    of *Kathleen, the Daughter of Houlahan.*

        The Signs:

Our priests and our nuns in unison pray.
The bones of our dead rot quietly away.
The sun is the face of a furnace fire
and the light of the moon is a tune on a lyre.
The heavens are covered with hammered gold
and the stars have increased a hundred fold.
All signs that freedom will soon be won
by none but the Royal Warrior Son
of *Kathleen, the Daughter of Houlahan.*

From 'THE CELTIC SURA'

i

Writing Out of Doors

'The forests' masts tower round about.
All manner of bird flies in and out;
the blackbirds' songs sound glad,
while I write in my shade.

That cuckoo calls my hours and quarters.
    He too wears a hood.
    Protect me Lord, all Saints and Martyrs
        to write well in my greenwood.'

ii

The Poet's Request

I ask
for a house
a small safe place,
not a hovel
for pigs and cattle;
wide open
with dignity in welcome
and a chair
well-cushioned with horsehair
at my desk.

iii

The Poet and his Dog

We pair work alone out here together
day after day in every kind of weather.
His job's to guard the kitchen from wild cats,
mine's to daily make my manuscripts.

More than town, or talk in public places,
I prefer the silence of my house's
study. He, wrapped round my feet, keeps both
us warm. And, because well fed, he's worth
his keep because he keeps those thieving cats
out of the larder of our common eats.
He sometimes growls in sleep about his dreams
while I am plotting literary schemes.
We both get on with what we must each day
which kills the joke of this life's unfair play.
He's master of his trade, devoted worker.
I'm pledged for life to mine and want no other.

An Ceangal

Then one Spring
The Viking . . .

Tonight the sea wind's high,
the wave's tip white spray;
tonight no fear of those who sail
the straight of our Irish channel.

An Ceangal

The sea, oh the sea
a grá geal mo chroí
long may it flow
between England and me.
It's a sure guarantee
that one day we'll be free
thank God we're surrounded by water.

Popular Irish Song